Through
Glimpses of old
Characters of
Dumfries and Galloway

Dumfries and Galloway Libraries,
Information and Archives
with Whithorn Photographic Group
1999

First published 1999
© Part text copyright Whithorn Photographic Group, Publication
copyright Dumfries and Galloway Council

Designed by Dumfries and Galloway Libraries, Information
and Archives. Set and printed by Solway Offset Services,
Catherinefield Industrial Estate, Dumfries for the publisher.

Dumfries and Galloway Libraries, Information and Archives
Central Support Unit, Catherine Street
Dumfries DG1 1JB

ISBN 0 946280 36 3
Characters of Dumfries and Galloway is number 12 in the
Dumfries and Galloway: Through the Lens series.
For a full list of our publications write to the above address.

ACKNOWLEDGEMENTS

For identifications of individuals and places: Mr
Donnie Nelson, Mr and Mrs McColm, Betty Stuart,
Mrs McLean, Mrs McGeoch.

For material: Dr Peter Hopkins, Lesley Parker, Miss
M McCormick, Mary McShane, Mr and Mrs A
Gladstone, Mr Andrew Ross, Mr J McLay, Dr Guy
Brown, Mrs J Gaw, Mr D Bell, Mrs E Drape, Dr
Smith, Mr and Mrs John McColm, Family of the late
Mrs W Anderson, Sybil Prentice, Dumfries &
Galloway Museum Services and John Adair.

INTRODUCTION

It may be as well to define the criteria we have used in selecting *characters* for this booklet. It falls into two unequal sections: in the first, we have included the *worthies* of towns and villages in Dumfries and Galloway, following the definition of *worthy* in Chambers' Dictionary as *local celebrity*. This automatically excluded those whose fame, because of some exceptional literary, scientific or military distinction, reached well beyond the boundaries of the region. In the second, shorter section, we have included some material on the gypsies, both tinkers and visiting Romany gypsies, who were a regular sight at their encampments in Dumfries and Galloway. The two sections have in common only that both groups existed on the margins of the regular society in the town, often scraped a living from itinerant selling, and both contributed to the richness, both cultural and visual, of life in the area, particularly up to the Second World War.

There is a notable literature on the worthies in Dumfries and Galloway, amounting almost to a minor literary genre: one thinks of John Drylie's **Worthies of Dumfriesshire and Galloway,** 1908, James T Cannon's **Droll Recollections of Whithorn and Vicinity,** 1904, Gordon Fraser's several books on the Wigtown area, Joseph Waugh's **Thornhill and its Worthies, 1923,** and the **Memorials of Sanquhar Kirkyard,** to name a selection. It may be that this explosion of literature came in the wake of the national popularity of Dean Ramsay's **Reminiscences of Scottish Life and Character,** 1858, which went through twenty-one editions in his lifetime.

This interest in the worthies may seem to us now a curious phenomenon, belonging to a strictly defined historical epoch. Yet the society which gave rise to and treasured the worthies emerges as a less sanitised environment than our own; more naive perhaps, but also more inclusive and less squeamish. Above all, it emerges as one which accepted and perhaps revelled in variety: most of the worthies were treated with a marked affection and their wit, often spiced with a certain rebelliousness against the authorities, was remembered and recorded. Many in this volume received newspaper obituaries on their deaths, some were even buried by public subscription and some worthies exploited their popularity by selling postcards of themselves.

Most of the literature from the beginning of this century begins with a lament that the worthies are dying out, a comment one hears frequently echoed today. Some of this is perhaps simply a fault of perspective, in that no generation can perhaps appreciate its own peculiarities or uniqueness. There is no doubt, however, that the generation of worthies represented in this book belong to a time when small town life was still vigorous, before social security or strong centralisation, when a labour-intensive economy allowed a diversity of occupations at unskilled level. Perhaps these pictures will remind us how common a sight tramps were on the road, and how a relatively immobile population was supported, exploited or enchanted by an army of pedlars, carters, beggars, strolling players, travelling sales people, and those who simply gathered the local news.

Without the individuals from Dumfries and Galloway who contributed photographs, the volume would not have been possible; without the dedication and hard work of my colleagues in Whithorn Photographic Group, it would never have appeared. Thanks are due to Lesley Murray, for collecting material, and to Jim Allan and Joe Whiteford for research and photographic printing.

Julia H Muir Watt,
Secretary, Whithorn Photographic Group

GROUP OF CHARACTERS, GEORGE STREET, STRANRAER
No names are recorded for this group exchanging news in the centre of Stranraer. the picture captures the flavour of more leisured times, as they stand in the middle of what is now a busy junction. Behind them is the George Hotel, built in 1876, but incorporating an earlier, eighteenth century, building. Its mansard roof and dormer windows give it a continental feel.

WILLIAM AND JAMES GARRET, STRANRAER, 1911
A photograph of these fishermen appeared in the Wigtownshire Free Press of May 4, 1911, when James Garret attained his hundredth year. He and his son, William (with the full beard and moustache), himself over 70, were celebrated as Scotland's oldest working fishermen and had fished from Loch Ryan all their lives. James Garret had been born at Innermessan in 1811, of parents from whom he obviously inherited his longevity: his mother and father lived to 100 and 103 respectively. A third generation of Garrets, in the person of William Garret junior, was also fishing at Stranraer. These men must have been some of many of the nautical characters, connected with the harbour and fishing industry in Stranraer, who could be seen daily round the Breastworks.

PAPER DAVIE, STRANRAER

Paper Davie was a familiar figure on the streets of Stranraer, where he made a living through the unlikely medium of selling out-of-date editions of the *Wigtown Free Press*. His distinctive sales cry, which began as soon as he left the Free Press offices, echoed through the streets. Here, he appears to be playing the mouth-organ, on the corner of Hanover Street, in about 1910?

BLIN' JOHNNIE, STRANRAER

Blin' Johnnie was a popular character in Stranraer, as is attested by this postcard picture of him playing the recorder. The sharpness of his other senses made up for his blindness, since he could recognise every passing farmer who was in town on business by his greeting. If he failed to identify an individual by hearing, he could accurately guess through coming close and smelling his clothing. He was buried at Inch churchyard and his memorial was raised by popular subscription. He receives a mention in a memoir by a locally born medical man, Professor McNeill, who wrote *Auld Lang Syne and the Rhins of Galloway.*

OLD NANCY, LOGAN HOUSE, PORT LOGAN

Miss Nancy Davidson was another centenarian, who died at Logan House on 30 December 1911; her obituary appears in the *Galloway Gazette* of January 14, 1911. Reportedly, she had come to Port Logan at the age of three, when her father came from Ireland as a labourer on the construction of the Logan pier. The pier was built ultimately in 1818-22 under the superintendence of John Young, after proposals had been put forward by John Rennie in 1814. *Old Nancy* came to be employed by the same family, the McDoualls of Logan and never left Kirkmaiden; her reminiscences, by the end of her long life, were a fascinating reminder of bygone times. Here she is pictured, probably on the lawns of Logan gardens, now owned by the Royal Botanic Gardens. Her costume is interesting: heavy boots, a linen apron over a skirt and a plaid shawl, with a mutch covering her hair and shadowing her face.

JOHN BAILLIE, ST. HELENA ISLAND, GLENLUCE
John Baillie, pictured here in about 1900 with his shotgun broken over his arm, was a seafaring man, who had visited and stayed on St. Helena island during his travels. When he settled on a small island on the shores of Luce Bay, he called his house *St Helena* and the name has remained. It is said that he brought shrubs and plants from St Helena, but tides and erosion have obliterated traces of his house and garden. He kept bees and farmed the land round the house, and gave employment to local villagers during the harvest. He went to Glenluce on business, using the right-of-way beside the River Luce. Some of his land now forms part of the County Golf club. His cottage must have resembled many in Galloway from the seventeenth century onwards, with its small windows, limewashed walls and its trimmed long-straw thatch, with horizontal sways to hold it down against the winds.

ROBBIE McWHINNIE, OR *RAB O' THE WHINS,* PORT WILLIAM AREA
Several postcard pictures of the *Galloway Giant,* Robbie McWhinnie, exist; this particular one is taken by the Wigtown photographer, Alan Nicolson, probably between 1905 and 1914. Robbie McWhinnie's height of 6 foot four inches seems hardly exceptional enough to justify his title, although accounts of it vary up to 7 foot 2 inches. In this picture, it is clear that most of his height was in his legs, since the trousers have pieces sewn in at the bottom. He seems to have worked occasionally as a chimney sweep, although he apparently also sold postcards (often of himself) from a pack; perhaps he is carrying packets of cards in this picture. He acquired the nickname *Rab O' the Whins* from his habit of sleeping rough in the countryside, under a whin bush.

RAB LOVE, PORT WILLIAM

Rob Love appears here with a "cuddy cart" in the Square, Port Willian; but he was often to be found with a hand cart, from which he sold fish, bought from the boats, during the summer months. The wicker basket on the cart is probably full of fish. During these months, he would go barefoot, like the children glimpsed behind him against the wall of McMaster's shop. During the winter, he was a stone napper and it is his handiwork which is represented in Port William's Free Kirk. Perhaps this trade accounted for his extraordinary strength; at any rate, he was reputed to be able single-handedly to lift a barrel of treacle from the ships, when they came into harbour. He lived in a small house, now demolished, behind Main Street, with his mother who was a washerwoman.

SANNY GRIFFIN, PORT WILLIAM
Judging by the numbers of portraits of Sanny Griffin, he must have been a popular figure in the district. He is pictured here at the Bottle Hole in Port William; some of the houses in the picture behind him have now been demolished. He had lodgings in a cottage where Mill Hill garage was built. The story is told of him that he left his donkey cart outside a house where he was visiting; while he was inside, children unhitched the animal from the trap and led it through a gate. They then re-hitched the trap to the donkey and left Sanny Griffin to puzzle as to how the animal had managed to pass through the bars of the gate.

JOHNNY LOGIE AT THE HERMIT'S CAVE, MONREITH

Like many of the characters in the book, Johnny Logie, here on the left, selected an unusual place to live: half-blinded in a mining accident in Ayrshire, he retreated to the cave now known as the Hermit's Cave and lived as self-sufficient a life as he could, raising vegetables in a garden on the shore. He received a pension after his accident and this was left for him in the dyke on the nearby road at Cairndoon. The cave mouth was built up with bits of driftwood, as can be seen, but was apparently dry and comfortable inside. He was a convinced Communist and had a portrait of Stalin on the wall of the hut. Locally he was well known, as is attested by the visit from two photographers: Sammy Roddie is the young man with the camera. Johnny Logie left the cave in 1962, shortly before his death. He was one of several cave dwellers round the shores of Luce Bay, though his stay in the cave was perhaps one of the longest.

11

ROBERT JOHN CONNING, WHITHORN

Pictured here outside Mrs. Jones's lodging house in High Street, Whithorn, now demolished, is Robert John Conning, who had a passion for religious disputation and quotation. He was known for walking the streets of the burgh, with his Bible open in his hands, though it was, more often than not, upside-down. Conning was a family name with a long history in Whithorn: they had been inn-keepers at the long-vanished *Red Lion* inn, in the centre of Whithorn, back into the eighteenth century and certainly until the 1850s.

WILLIAM BLACK, TOWN CRIER, 1920s

William or *Wow* Black is also a household name in Whithorn, not least because three generations of Blacks held the office of town crier and gravedigger. The father of the William Black in this picture had been sexton at the Priory Church during the 1880s excavations by William Galloway, under the patronage of the 3rd Marquess of Bute. Mr Galloway often had case to feel what powers belonged to the sexton, as he sought to dig in his domain. A picture of the sexton, who held the position for forty years, appears in James Cannon's *Droll Recollections of Whithorn and Vicinity* of 1904. William Black, his son, is pictured here with the town bell at a sports day on Priory Croft during the 1920s.

WILLIAM HOOD, alias *WULLIE HUDE,* WHITHORN
This picture comes from James Cannon's 1904 book on Whithorn worthies and was taken by William Hawthorn, Agent of the National Bank of Scotland in Whithorn, It is probably taken to the rear of the Bank premises. Wullie Hude, who died shortly after the turn of the century, appears to have been harmless and mild-tempered, though remarkably hardy and strong: he was known for running barefoot after the coaches, which would have plied to and from the town. Despite the perpetual bare feet, he liked to dress respectably and attend funerals. He was also known for a weird screeching, known locally as the *Sorbie lauch* and for making his own instruments out of sticks to accompany his singing.

JAMES *FLUKE* MILROY, WHITHORN

James Milroy, called *Fluke* apparently because of a tendency of his mouth to move from side to side, was an Irishman by origin and, like many Irish immigrants, had to make a living on the margins of society. According to a local poem of over a dozen verses entitled *Fluke's Cart,* the name was given him by local youths who would torment him with it when he sold fish from an old cart, which was kept in a shed at the *Back Ra'* behind the High Street. According to James Cannon, he also kept an accommodation house *for vagrants and nondescripts.* The top hat was apparently a trademark, since the rhyme reads *Wi' a real jaunty bash in his hat an' a dash/Sic as Eerish folk hae, at ance ceevil and pert.*

CHARLES McKIE AND ANDREW KINNEAR, WHITHORN
Pictured here on the corner of King's Road are Charlie Kie, (left) who had a most unusual home at the Windmill Stump, Whithorn and rode a tricycle about the town. The second man in the picture, Andrew Kinnear, who is propped against the wall, lived in Isle Street and used a stick after suffering a crippling bout of rheumatic fever.

ONE-LEGGED CHARACTER, WHITHORN
The only clue to this gentleman's name is given in the verse which surrounds the original postcard:-

Will you share with me your fortune,
Shure now Nettie tell me plain.
I'm a singer from dear old Ireland,
and Paddy is my name.
How soon we could our fortune make
With you at the doors to thump,
And bring the coppers round to me
For mind I have a stump.

JEAN DUNLOP, WIGTOWN

Some residents of Wigtown will still remember the kindly figure of Jean Dunlop, with her characteristic shuffling gait, who lived in Wigtown until her death at some time in the 1930s. She had a house in the High Street, now demolished, and carried out casual work on farms, such as cleaning out hen-houses, as she is pictured here. She wears heavy hand-made boots, as many working women did, a striped dress with flannel petticoats, and a shawl with a gathered trim.

UNKNOWN CHARACTER WITH FIDDLE, WIGTOWN
This travelling player, with his rough collie and fiddle, would visit Wigtown every year for the Agricultural Show, where he would play at the gate. Here he is pictured in Harbour Road with his back to the Inks, the tidal marshes on Wigtown Bay. Many itinerant entertainers would visit agricultural shows: at one time, perhaps up until the 1940s, there would be side-shows including escape-artists, chain-swallowers and illusionists. Earlier still, the stalls and shows would also be laid on in Wigtown's main square.

SINGA McGOWAN, WIGTOWN

Singa McGowan caught and sold flounders through the burgh of Wigtown. He wears the fisherman's characteristic waterproof boots, but the umbrella is less explicable, given the apparently dry conditions. At one point, there were stake nets in Wigtown Bay, to which certain fisherman had rights, and where flounders were caught. He is pictured here in the main square of Wigtown.

KECK FINNIGAN, WIGTOWN, 1915

Keck Finnigan lived in the High Vennel, Wigtown in a one-room cottage. He is pictured here, perched on the window-sill of a newsagent's in the town square, pointing towards a sandwich board, on which can just be glimpsed the news of the train disaster at Quintinshill. This took place on 22 May 1915, near Gretna, when a troop train, crowded with volunteers from the 7th Battalion Royal Scots, ploughed into a local train, which had been dangerously positioned on the wrong line, when allowing through a north-bound express. All three trains ended up in a catastrophic collision, which claimed 227 lives, all but nine of which were among the troops. *Keck* himself is not known to have had any connection with the disaster, although the news doubtless struck home nationwide. Interestingly, the name *Keck* seems to have belonged to other worthies; it is apparently meant someone of small stature. Other tramp names, like *Snib* (Snib Scott of the South Machars and the later Snib Scott of Ballantrae) also seem to have belonged to more than one individual; sometimes, like *Fluke Milroy,* the name was inherited by the next generation.

DUNDEE ANNIE, WIGTOWN AREA

It is not known why *Dundee* Annie acquired that sobriquet: she seems to have lived most of her life as a tramp, often visiting the Wigtown area, although sometimes straying as far as the Stewartry. She probably lived by begging for scraps and the occasional drink. Tramps were a much more frequent sight than they are now: after World War I, many injured or shell-shocked men took to the roads and begged. The peripatetic tramps like Dundee Annie were distinguished from the burgh *worthies,* who, though sometimes eccentric or even disreputable, were an accepted part of the town scene, while the tramps were entirely outside society.

ROBBIE *DEARIE*, NEWTON STEWART

Robert Brown, who came to be known as Robbie Dearie, was a familiar figure on the roads around Newton Stewart, until his death in December 1940; his obituary is in the *Galloway Gazette* of 14 December. He was born in 1873 and had lived with an uncle on Barrhill farm, until that was sold upon his uncle's death. Thereafter, he moved first to a derelict building in Newton Stewart, where he carried on a rag-and-bone business, and then to the refuse dump near Barbuchany, where he made a house out of the available debris. Ultimately, a local businessman gave him corrugated shed, which was about seven foot square and had a door and window, but was patched with rags and rubbish from the dump. He was partially blind, but nonetheless made two weekly shopping trips, one to Kirkcowan on a Monday and to Wigtown on a Friday. It is likely that he survived on handouts from individuals or businesses.

JOCK BYRON, NEWTON STEWART

John Byron, alias *Jock,* is pictured here in about 1900; he was probably about forty years of age, since he appears in the 1891 Census as living in a house in Queen Street, aged 32, with his mother Isabella, who had seven children in all. He appears here standing by the decorative fountain which was in Dashwood Square until 1940. Like another Newton Stewart character, Willie Moffat, or *Black Sheep,* of whom another picture exists taken at exactly this location, possibly on the same day, Jock Byron was sufficiently well-known and popular to make postcard views of him saleable in the town.

BIDDY CAIN, PALNURE

Biddy Cain is seen standing here, outside her now-vanished thatched cottage at the roadside at Palnure. The sign advertises her home-made toffee and clove balls. The sweets were sold from trays, which were laid out on a white sheet, which covered her bed; the toffee was made in long twists, which would be cut to order for customers. Her husband, Henry, would deliver toffee by bicycle. Her produce was sufficiently celebrated to attract customers from as far afield at Hong Kong and the United States and many returned, year after year.

ELDERLY LADY, GATEHOUSE

We do not know the identity or age of this characterful lady from Gatehouse, but her thickened fingers and rugged lines bespeak a long life of hard work and clearly caught the attention of the photographer. In an era when fashions and fabrics changed far less and when specific modes of dress were assigned according to age and gender, she wears the costume typical of an elderly working woman: a traditional shawl of checked shepherd's plaid, frilled mutch to cover her hair, and high starched apron.

JOHN HOUSTON, KIRKCUDBRIGHT

A genuine lad o' pairts, John was a rural postman based in Kirkcudbright, who had lost an arm as a result of an early farming accident. He became nationally known as the *Weather Prophet,* whose forecasts based solely on observation of the changing skies, were published in national newspapers. When a bride-to-be asked him about the likely weather for her wedding day, he replied *Buy the Evening Times, Miss, and you will get your information for a half-penny.* He was also a prominent sportsman, who at cricket bowled well enough to bring praise from the famous A G Steele in the 1880s, was captain of Kirkcudbright Football Team, an excellent runner of the mile and a fine draughts and chess player. As an inventor he produced items as varied as a *Time Gun* for ending football matches and an automatic coupler for railway engines. To cap it all he was considered the finest rodent exterminator in the district.

JEN DOUGLAS, KIRKCUDBRIGHT, 1900

The personality of this Kirkcudbright character captured the eye of one of the earliest photographers in the town, Robert McConchie, who was a member of an old-established local family of clothiers in St Mary's Street; the shop was a gathering-place for Kirkcudbright artists. He apparently travelled the countryside with his photographic equipment loaded on his bicycle. It is tantalising to think that many glass plate negatives, perhaps of this quality, were destroyed in the 1930's. Jen Douglas was known to be a woman of some wit and education, though she was equally noted for her eccentricities: it is reported that, immediately after her husband's death, when he was laid out in the house, she was found eating her breakfast using the lid of the coffin as a convenient table. The clay pipe, however, is not a personal idiosyncrasy: they were frequently smoked by countrywomen and Thomas Carlyle records that when he revisited his Dumfriesshire home, he and his mother sat by the fire, comfortably smoking their pipes together.

The article below from the Kirkcudbrightshire Advertiser of 12 March 1897, probably relates to the accompanying photograph.

…Many people alive will remember Joe Summers - that long, lank, hanging-headed being whose proudest possession was a *duddy bane wi' flesh on't*. Then there was Joe Adams, whose distinguishing badge was a time-worn tall hat. I have before me, as I write, a photograph of those two worthies standing at the iron pump which used to be outside the wall of *Stewart's Photographic Saloon*, where Gladstone Place now joins St Mary Street.

JOHNNY SINCLAIR, KIRKCUDBRIGHT

Johnny Sinclair, who was born in Kirkcudbright High Street in September 1822 and died in September 1888, became a favourite in the town, owing to his being rather weak-minded and unable to fend for himself or earn a living. It is said that he saved the life of the local minister, Rev John Underwood, who looked after him during his lifetime. His funeral was attended by a number of influential citizens, of whom Mr George Hamilton FSA, a local antiquarian, paid for a tombstone to be erected in St Cuthbert's Cemetery.

WILLIAM CUNNINGHAM JNR., SANQUHAR

He continued his father's business as a Sanquhar watch and clock maker, but it was through his prowess as a pedestrian that he achieved local fame. His business often took him to Glasgow, and before the railway came he would walk the 48 miles over the moors; once he bet the coach driver that he could beat the stage-coach, and did so by twenty minutes. He also walked the 26.5 miles to Dumfries in under four hours. There is a Cunningham longcase clock in Sanquhar Museum to commemorate the feats of William who died in 1880 at the age of 67.

MRS GOLOGLY, DUMFRIES c1930

Mrs Gologly and her shop was a Dumfries institution for 50 years, the secondhand goods (some would now be valuable antiques) overflowing unto the street. Her husband Owen had started a brokerage business in Brewery Street by 1882, and had opened the shop at the foot of the Rainbow Stairs (at the rear of the Tolbooth) by 1892. After he died in 1910 Mary, his widow, continued the business until the early 'thirties when the Tolbooth was demolished to make was for Burton's the Tailors. The family dynasty was continued by Mary's daughter Winnie, who had a confectioner's business on Academy Street.

TARRY LARRY, DUMFRIES

Lawrence Murphy derived his nickname from his last profession, that of tarring buildings and fences around Dumfries, but he'd already achieved fame from his earlier varied career. When a boy, he went on errands for frogs and hedgehogs for the French prisoners-of-war and spent the next fifty years on the Atlantic Shipping Trade until "the very dogs in Quebec knew him". On his retirement to Dumfries he continued his nautical pursuits by rafting timber on the Nith, and saved several people from drowning in the river. He retained great physical strength into his old age; in Dumfries Poorhouse at the age of 98 he conceived a dislike for an Irish 88-year-old, and asked the governor for *five meenits o' Jimmy McInroe ootside*. He died in 1902 aged 101.

TAM BROON, MAXWELLTOWN
An inveterate poacher from his early days, Tam was born in Maxwelltown. When still a boy he claimed the Procurator Fiscal's reward for finding the culprit who'd taken apples from his, the Fiscal's, orchard. Upon receiving an assurance that the thief would not be prosecuted Tam took the money and revealed the villain's identity - himself! Tam was often jailed for his activities although on one occasion his *sagacious dog* saved him by running back with *news* of a police ambush. Tam was not always teetotal, and said this about his own fame; *Gang up the Vennel and cry Tam Broon has a croon in his pooch* and naebody'll believe ye, but say *Tam Broon's drunk and naebody'll doot ye*. Tam died in 1895, but not until he'd read his own obituary notice, published somedays too soon.

JEAN BRAND, THE BLIND FIDDLER, AND BIDDIE OF DUMFRIES, c1870

Jean Brand, pictured here in a long green and black checked waterproof coat, which was her trademark, and her scoop bonnet, was a well-known figure in Dumfries, where she lived in a lane off College Street, Maxwellton. Like many entertainers, she travelled widely, from the Stewartry to Annandale, to fairs, markets and houses of the gentry, to receive charity in exchange for her performance on the fiddle. Jean could not in fact play a note, and an unearthly screeching was the result, but she kept time to her *music* by screwing her mouth up with each upstroke of the bow. Biddy was perpetually knitting grey stockings and had a fierce demeanour which was useful for subduing high-spirited youths. They lived, when not travelling, at College Street, Maxwelltown.

JOHNNIE MORGAN, KIRKCONNEL

Johnnie was a wandering hawker, originating from Kirkconnel, who sold scythe sand, hones, walking sticks and keel for farmers in Dumfries and the Stewartry. Tommy, his donkey, and Quharrie, his dog, were inseparable companions, although to the rest of the world Johnnie could appear gruff and discontented. The only compliment he is ever supposed to have made was to the Burgh Council of Sanquhar: the new pillar lamps they had erected were a great improvement because he could tether his donkey to them. He was once asked how old his donkey was and said *it was three year old when I got it, and I've had it ever since.* He was thought to be the original of S R Crockett's *Silver Sand,* and died in Upper Nithsdale Poorhouse in 1901.

TAFFY MARY, MONIAIVE

Mary Ann Williamson or Walsh was a hawker of toffee (taffy), oranges and apples in Mid-Nithsdale. She lived in Moniaive, and was well known for her lack of temperance. She always carried a small bottle of whisky to *slocken her thirst,* and sometimes became quite incapacitated. The following morning she might be found sleeping on the road or in a ditch, a burn or even fallen down a hole. A religious friend attempted to frighten her by asking *Do you know where all drunkards go? Aweel* said Mary *I dinna ken whaur they a' gang, but I gang tae Currie's; I get the best stuff there.* Her sad death was as a result not of drinking, but smoking; she set her bedclothes on fire one night in 1894 and died mostly of shock.

KIRSTY RULE, ANNAN
Kirsty Rule's occupation as water-carrier in Annan is an interesting reflection on the way in which different levels of technology allow different possibilities of employment; in the 1870s when Kirsty Rule was a well known character in Annan, a labour-intensive economy enabled many people to earn a living in occupations requiring little but physical strength and endurance. Note the circular hoop, which keeps the buckets away from her legs when walking. The water was delivered to town houses for washing purposes. She wears wooden clogs. She lived in a house in Bruce Street with her mother and apparently like many on the margins of society, had much to put up with in the way of torment from local youths. They would shout *Where's the bairn ye buried in the ashpit* or *Daft Kirsty ran awa' wi' the besom man.* Kirsty died in the poorhouse.

GYPSY ENCAMPMENT AT THE SNAP INN, c1890

The picture shows a typical gypsy encampment, with its canvas covered wagons, horses and the rising smoke of a fire. The Snap Inn was at The Knowe village, often simply known as *The Snap*. Gypsy camp grounds were hallowed by long tradition: they existed at Whithorn, at *Mushy Morton* outside Wigtown, at Creetown, Minnigaff, and at the Dhoon and Nunmill, near Kirkcudbright. The tinkler-gypsies were associated with horse-trading, repair of pots and pans, and sale of small household goods.

VISITING ENGLISH GYPSIES IN GALLOWAY

This picture appeared in Andrew McCormick's book *The Tinkler Gypsies of Galloway:* McCormick was remarkable in combining the offices of solicitor in Newton Stewart and Provost of the town, while also in being a gypsiologist of distinction. He spoke Romany and avidly collected records of tinkler's cant words. He contributed to government investigations of conditions amongst the gpsies, and his records of conversations with gypsies and tinkers encamped round Newton Stewart are now invaluable sources for gypsy studies. This picture hung on the wall of his legal offices in Newton Stewart for many years; it gives a good close-up view of an individual family encamped. The tent was known as a *wattle* and could be taken apart and put into a sack to be carried on the back. McCormick took some trouble to differentiate the English, Irish, Welsh and continental gypsies from each other and from the tinkers, and to map their characteristic family names and the differences and similarities in vocabulary used by them.

ENGLISH GYPSY CHILDREN NEAR CREETOWN

This photograph too appears in the *Tinkler Gypsies* and was taken on a visit by Andrew McCormick to an encampment of English gypsies, named Chumomistos, near Creetown. In this case, he showed the gypsy girls a story from *In Gypsy Tents* by Francis Groome, called *Happy Bozzle;* the children are reading sitting on the steps of their painted horse-drawn caravan. The interest in gypsies and in their language had been stimulated by the popularity of George Borrow's *Lavengro* and *Romany Rye,* which had led to a flood of gypsy literature at the end of the nineteenth century. McCormick himself wrote an article on George Borrow's trip to Galloway; he was in contact with most of the distinguished gypsiologists of his day.

GYPSIES AT THE DHOON, KIRKCUDBRIGHT

This is one of several gypsy scenes taken in the 1890s by Kirkcudbright photographer Robert McConchie, in the town's environs: in this case, at the Dhoon on the western shore of Kirkcudbright Bay. It looks as if the cart is of the sort known as a *pot cart,* so called because it originated with gypsies trading in cheap pottery and was used for display and also as a base for a demountable tent. Eventually the tent top became a permanent fixture and might be mounted on a four wheeled cart, and was finally replaced by a wooden superstructure, which could house comforts such as a stove, bunks and cupboards. The oldest woman in the group faces the camera, while the other resolutely turn their backs: as Andrew McCormick's accounts prove, obtaining gypsy pictures was a matter of negotiation and becoming acquainted with the subjects.